BACKPACK EXPLORER

BIRD WATCH

Storey Publishing

Are You Ready for a BIRD WATCH ADVENTURE?

You can see birds in lots of places! Look for them while you're playing outside, going on a hike, or having a picnic in the park. You're sure to see them if you keep your eyes open and your ears alert.

THINGS TO BRING ON A BIRD WATCH

Binoculars

Backpack

Camera

Bug spray

A pen or pencil and this book

Snacks

Water bottle

Sunscreen

HOW TO HAVE FUN WITH THIS BOOK!

Listen for BIRD CALLS

Look for FEATHERS

Use the MAGNIFYING GLASS

Build a NEST

Play bird GAMES

Search for FLYING, PERCHING, and SWIMMING birds

Fill out your BIRD WATCH LIST

Read FUN FACTS

BIRD WATCH BADGES

Look for the 12 sticker badges at the end of this book. Each one matches an **I SEE IT!** circle on a Field Guide page. When you spot a bird or bird sign from an **I SEE IT!** page, put the sticker on the matching circle.

I SEE IT!

FIELD GUIDE
Nests & Eggs

A NEST IS A SAFE SPOT WHERE A BIRD LAYS ITS EGGS. Nests can be made out of dry grass, sticks, pine needles, moss, or mud. You may find them on a tree branch, hidden in a bush, or stuck under a roof. Some nests sit on the ground. Cavity nests are tucked inside tree trunks, birdhouses, or even cactuses!

Some birds lay just 2 or 3 eggs. Others lay more than 20!

Robin's eggs

Have you seen any of these kinds of **NESTS**?

Barn swallows mix mud and grass to build nests.

Barn Swallow

Osprey

The number of eggs in a nest is called a **clutch**.

Gila Woodpecker

Some birds line their nests with soft feathers.

American Crow

Canada Goose

If you were a bird, what kind of nest would you build?

Zoom In — Look for an abandoned nest in bushes or low branches. Can you tell what materials the bird used to make it?

19

Bird Watch
TIPS

Here are some ways to find feathered friends.

PICK A SPOT TO STAND AND WATCH PATIENTLY for a few minutes. When you're still, you see more birds.

LISTEN QUIETLY FOR BIRD CALLS.
Close your eyes and notice the sounds around you.

DON'T GET TOO CLOSE
to a bird on the ground.

LOOK AT THE BIRD'S SIZE, SHAPE, AND COLOR
to help identify it.

FOLLOW FLYING BIRDS WITH YOUR EYES.
You might see them go to their nest or find something to eat.

Singing & Perching Birds

I SEE IT!

SONGBIRDS MAY COME IN DIFFERENT SHAPES AND COLORS, BUT THEY ALL LOVE TO SING. They have special voice boxes in their throats for making whistles, chirps, and trills. Males do most of the singing, to attract mates and to defend their home territory. They love to show off!

Songbird chicks learn to sing by listening to the adults around them while they are still in the nest.

Western Meadowlark

Can you HEAR birds singing?

Black-capped Chickadee

Does the sound of singing birds wake you up in the morning?

House Finch

American Robin

Chipping Sparrow

Try making up your own song!

House Wren

Eastern Bluebird

What is your favorite birdsong? Can you imitate it?

Northern Mockingbird

Eastern Phoebe

Baby birds learn to sing from their parents.

Tufted Titmouse

Scarlet Tanager

Zoom In

Songbirds perch on branches by gripping with their feet. They have three forward toes and one backward toe. Compare that to your own feet!

Make a BIRDFEEDER

Hang up a couple of different ones and see who comes to visit!

PEANUT BUTTER SEED TREATS

1 Mix 1 cup of peanut butter with 1 cup of birdseed.

2 Cut a small pumpkin, apple, or orange in half. Hollow out the middle of each piece.

3 Fill the hollow fruit with the seed mixture. Pack it tight!

4 Tie a long piece of twine to the stem (or wrap it around the fruit) and hang it from a branch or birdfeeder station.

TASTY GARLAND

1 Gather a mix of food that is good for birds: dried fruit, slices of apple or orange, grapes, plain air-popped popcorn, peanuts in the shell.

2 Have an adult thread a thick needle with heavy thread or fishing line.

3 Push the needle and thread through the pieces of food like you're making a necklace.

NOTE: Bread, crackers, and sugary cereal aren't healthy food for birds.

BAG OF NUTS

This one's super easy! Just fill mesh onion or produce bags with sunflower seeds or unsalted, shelled peanuts, almonds, or other nuts.

You can also smear the peanut butter and seed mixture on a pinecone or dried corncob.

Tie your tasty garlands to a tree branch.

Add sticks for perching birds.

Colorful Birds

FEATHERS COME IN JUST ABOUT ANY COLOR YOU CAN IMAGINE, from soft browns and grays to bright red, orange, and blue. Bright feathers attract attention — they say, "Look at me, I'm strong and healthy!" Duller colors help a bird blend in with its surroundings and hide from predators while sitting on its nest.

Many birds, like bluebirds, are named for their colorful feathers. Can you think of some other birds with blue feathers?

Eastern Bluebird

How many **DIFFERENT COLORS** of birds can you see?

Ruby-throated Hummingbird

Baltimore Oriole

American Goldfinch

Northern Cardinal

If you were a bird, what color would you like to be?

Tree Swallow

Have you ever seen a striped feather or one with spots?

Rufous Hummingbird

Monk Parakeet

Indigo Bunting

What colorful birds are in your neighborhood?

Painted Bunting

American Flamingo

Scarlet Tanager

Zoom In

Iridescent [ihr-uh-DEH-suhnt] feathers seem to glow in the light and look metallic.

FABULOUS FEATHERS

ALL BIRDS, EVEN ONES THAT CAN'T FLY, HAVE FEATHERS. That sets them apart from all other animals in the world. Lightweight, flexible, and strong, feathers are important for lots of reasons.

Keeping cozy and warm

Staying dry

Hiding

Flying

Attracting a mate

EACH TYPE OF FEATHER HAS A JOB.

Long, strong **wing feathers** arranged in rows allow the bird to fly.

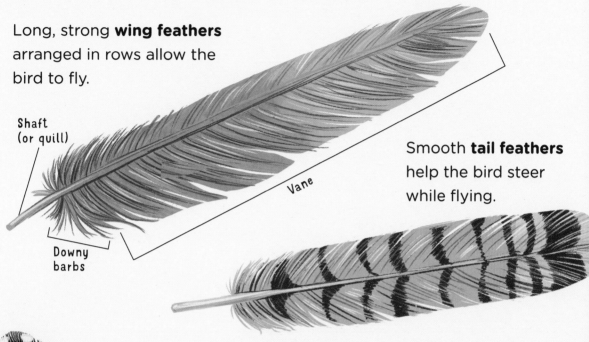

Shaft (or quill)

Vane

Downy barbs

Smooth **tail feathers** help the bird steer while flying.

Contour feathers cover a bird's body, giving it shape and color.

Fluffy **down feathers** are next to the skin for extra warmth.

Soft **semiplume feathers** help keep a bird warm.

Some birds have short, stiff **bristle feathers** for feeling things near their eyes and beaks.

FIELD GUIDE
Woodpeckers

WOODPECKERS USE THEIR STRONG, POINTED BEAKS TO DRILL HOLES INTO TREE TRUNKS. They poke their long tongues into the holes to snatch up tasty insects. They also dig out holes large enough to nest in. Pileated Woodpeckers sometimes make their holes so big they accidentally break a tree in half!

Woodpeckers call, but they don't really sing. Instead, they drum their beaks on hard wood or metal to make loud noises to say, "I'm here!"

Hairy Woodpecker

Where is that **DRUMMING SOUND** coming from?

Red-headed Woodpecker

Downy Woodpecker

Acorn woodpeckers stash acorns in the holes they drill.

Acorn Woodpecker

Can you drum like a woodpecker?

Pileated Woodpecker

Northern Flicker

Northern flickers mostly eat ants off the ground.

Red-bellied Woodpecker

Zoom In

A tree trunk full of holes probably means woodpeckers are around. Are the holes square or round? Are they in rows? Can you fit a finger in one?

LISTEN UP!

Sometimes it's easier to hear a bird than to see one. Close your eyes and listen to the sounds around you. Do you hear any of these things?

- ☐ Chirping chicks
- ☐ Bird singing in a tree
- ☐ Cawing crow
- ☐ Drumming woodpecker

- ☐ Quacking duck
- ☐ Honking goose
- ☐ Cry of a hawk
- ☐ Buzzing hummingbird wings

LEARNING BiRD CALLS

Most birds use their voices to send messages to each other.

A **SONG** is a pattern of short or long notes that sound like music. Birds sing to attract a mate or defend their home, mostly in winter and spring.

A **CALL** is one or more short notes repeated a few times. Calls can mean "I'm here! Where are you?" or "Feed me!" or "Look out!"

Some birds mimic the sounds other birds make, and you can, too! Try copying these:

Chickadee

CHICKADEE-DEE-DEE-DEE

WHOOO-COOKS-FOR-YOOOU?

Barred Owl

CONK-LA-LEEEEE

HOO-AH HOO HOO HOO

HOO-AH HOO HOO HOO

Red-winged Blackbird

KEEEEEEEEEEEEEEEEERRR!

Red-tailed Hawk

Mourning Dove

Ravens, Crows & Jays

I SEE IT!

RAVENS, CROWS, AND JAYS ARE SOME OF THE SMARTEST ANIMALS ON THE PLANET. They have great memories, like to play tricks, can teach each other new skills, and even make tools out of sticks! Some mimic the calls of other birds, and captive ravens have learned to say human words.

Steller's Jay

Steller's Jays have been known to imitate hawks, squirrels, cats, dogs, and even chickens.

Have you ever heard **NOISY CROWS** or jays calling?

American Crow

Ravens can fly upside down!

Ravens are much larger than crows, with longer middle tail feathers.

Canada Jay

Common Raven

Magpies may take over a month to build a big stick nest.

Black-billed Magpie

Blue Jay

Jays are social birds who like to hang out together.

Pinyon Jay

Zoom In

In the winter, crows gather together in large groups called **roosts**.

Nests & Eggs

A NEST IS A SAFE SPOT WHERE A BIRD LAYS ITS EGGS. Nests can be made out of dry grass, sticks, pine needles, moss, or mud. You may find them on a tree branch, hidden in a bush, or stuck under a roof. Some nests sit on the ground. Cavity nests are tucked inside tree trunks, birdhouses, or even cactuses!

Some birds lay just 2 or 3 eggs. Others lay more than 20!

Robin's eggs

Have you seen any of these kinds of **NESTS**?

Barn swallows mix mud and grass to build nests.

Barn Swallow

Osprey

The number of eggs in a nest is called a **clutch**.

Gila Woodpecker

American Crow

Some birds line their nests with soft feathers.

Canada Goose

If you were a bird, what kind of nest would you build?

Zoom In

Look for an abandoned nest in bushes or low branches. Can you tell what materials the bird used to make it?

BUILD A NEST

Just like a bird, you can make a cozy nest out of almost anything. Your nest can be as big or small, and as simple or fancy as you like. Try making one small enough to fit in your hand and one big enough to sit in!

1 Collect a pile of dried grasses, sticks, leaves, moss, milkweed or cottonwood fluff, pine needles, ribbons, yarn, rope, and other interesting materials.

2 Most nests are shaped like a circle. Weave your supplies into a bowl-like shape. A little mud might help things stick together!

3 When you have the shape you like, line your nest with soft moss or dandelion fluff.

If you're at the beach, dig a hole in the sand or mud and line it with seaweed or grasses to make a ground nest!

Imagine building a
nest with just a beak,
instead of two hands!

Ducks & Geese

I SEE IT!

DUCKS, GEESE, AND OTHER WATER BIRDS USUALLY HANG OUT ON PONDS AND LAKES. They swim around on top of the water using their wide, flat feet as paddles. Some dive down to nibble on plants, insects, or small fish. Others just dip down and tip their bottoms in the air. That's called **dabbling!**

Most water birds build their nests on the ground, so watch where you step near a wetland!

Common Loon

What kinds of birds do you see **IN** or **NEAR** water?

Blue-winged Teal

Snow Goose

Bread and cereal are bad for birds' tummies! Try corn, peas, oats, or greens instead.

Webbed feet are made for swimming!

Common Merganser

Canvasback

Can you find a water bird with a rounded beak? What about a pointy one?

Try quacking like a duck or honking like a goose!

Mallard

Canada Goose

Mute Swan

Bufflehead

Zoom In

A duck's footprint looks almost diamond-shaped. Can you see the webbing between its three toes?

BILL & FEET MATCHUP

Draw a line to match each bird's head to its feet.

Long & Sharp Bill
To spear or catch fish

Sandhill Crane

Flipper-like feet to paddle in the water
Swimming Feet

Rounded Bill
To strain plants and insects from the water

Mute Swan

Toes face in two directions to cling onto tree trunks
Climbing Feet

Sharp & Strong Bill
To hammer holes into tree trunks

Red-bellied Woodpecker

Big feet with long toes to keep from sinking in the mud
Wading Feet

Birds don't have teeth, so their beaks (also called bills) are made to find and catch their food. The shape of a bird's beak can tell you a lot about what it eats. So can its feet!

Hooked Bill

To catch and tear apart prey

Golden Eagle

Flexible toes to grasp branches and keep from falling

Perching Feet

Long & Slender Bill

To probe flowers and suck nectar

Rufous Hummingbird

Movable toes to move around on the ground

Hopping Feet

Short & Wide Bill

To pick berries and crack seeds

House Sparrow

Strong feet with sharp talons to catch and carry prey

Grasping Feet

Wading Birds

I SEE IT!

BIRDS WITH LONG, THIN LEGS ARE OFTEN WADING BIRDS. Their special legs and long toes help these birds balance in muddy wetlands and along fresh- and saltwater shores. Many also have long bills and long necks to reach the water to spear a fish or frog.

Great Blue Heron

Herons stand super still waiting for the right moment to strike their prey!

Look for **WADING BIRDS** at the edges of ponds and lakes.

Most of these birds can walk just one day after they hatch!

Great Egret

Spotted Sandpiper

American Avocet

Some wading birds nest in large groups called rookeries.

American Bittern

Sandhill Crane

Greater Yellowlegs

Roseate Spoonbill

What's your favorite wading bird?

American Oystercatcher

Green Heron

Zoom In

Imagine swallowing your dinner whole, like an egret or heron does!

Bird Food

YOU CAN FIND ALL SORTS OF DIFFERENT BIRD FOODS, DEPENDING ON THE SEASON. Flowers provide nectar for hummingbirds, trees drop seeds and nuts, and berry bushes offer sweet treats. Look under leaves and on tree trunks for insect snacks. You may even spot a mouse that's perfect for a hawk's lunch!

Ruby-throated Hummingbird

Put up different types of bird feeders to attract the most birds.

What do birds **EAT?**

Berries

Slugs

Have you seen robins looking for worms in the grass?

Worms

Beetles

Mollusks

Spiders

Acorns

Rodents

Crickets

What bird foods do you like eating? Which sound yucky?

Amphibians

Nectar

Seeds

Crayfish

Flies

Plants

Birds have different bills for eating different foods. (See page 24.)

Zoom In

Robins turn their heads to listen for worms rustling underground. Then they pounce!

WHAT'S FOR BREAKFAST?

Some birds eat seeds and fruit. Some eat insects. Some eat other animals. Some will eat just about anything! Follow the colored lines to see what these birds like to eat.

Cedar Waxwing

Nuthatch

Bald Eagle

Woodpeckers

Great Blue Heron

Hummingbirds

Hooded Merganser

Raptors

OWLS, HAWKS, EAGLES, AND OTHER HUNTING BIRDS, OR BIRDS OF PREY, ARE CALLED RAPTORS. **Fast and fierce, they have excellent eyesight and can spot small mammals and fish from high above. Most raptors dive through the air and grab their prey with their powerful feet and sharp talons.**

Hawks and eagles are **diurnal** [dy-UR-nuhl] and only hunt during the day. But most owls are **nocturnal** [nok-TUR-nuhl], or active at night.

Barred Owl

Can you see a **HAWK** or **TURKEY VULTURE** high in the sky?

Have you ever heard an owl hooting at night?

Barn Owl

Golden Eagle

Turkey vultures soar high in the air in big circles.

Vulture

The word **raptor** comes from a word meaning "to grasp or grab."

Northern Harrier

Most owls don't make noise when they fly.

Great Horned Owl

Red-tailed Hawk

Zoom In

Raptors have a sharp hook on the end of their beaks for tearing their food.

WATCH AN OWL GROW

Follow the pictures to see how a Great Horned Owl grows from egg to adult.

A mama **OWL** lays her eggs in her nest.

She sits on her **EGGS** until they hatch about 30 days later.

The father owl brings food to the mother while she sits on the eggs.

The helpless **CHICKS** don't open their eyes for another ten days.

YOUNG OWLS stay with their parents for several months until they are ready to live on their own.

The **OWLETS** get bigger every day, growing feathers until they are strong enough to fly.

PARTS OF A BIRD

From wing to tail and bill to feet, get to know the parts of a bird!

Head

Ear

Wing

Tail

Bill
(or beak)

Ankle

Leg

Toes

Ground Birds

GROUND BIRDS LIKE WILD TURKEYS, PHEASANTS, AND QUAIL MOSTLY GET AROUND BY WALKING. They can run and fly when they need to, but spend most of their time looking for berries, seeds, nuts, plants, and insects to eat off the ground. Chicks are ready to walk soon after hatching and follow their mamas all summer.

Northern Bobwhite

A group of partridges, quails, or similar birds is called a **covey** [KUH-vee].

What kind of **GROUND BIRDS** can you see?

When a grouse beats its wings it sounds like a motor running!

Wild Turkey

Ruffed Grouse

California Quail

Gray Partridge

A roadrunner can run 20 miles per hour!

Greater Roadrunner

Greater Sage Grouse

Ring-necked Pheasant

If you spot a flock of ground birds, try counting them.

Zoom In

The flap of skin hanging from a turkey's neck is called a **wattle**. Its bright red color helps the bird attract mates.

BiRD GAMES!

Pretend to be a bird! Try some of these simple games to get moving and have some fun.

WHOOO AM i?

Have one player think of a bird while the others ask yes-or-no questions to try to guess that bird. The player who guesses the right bird gets to think of the next one.

FOR EXAMPLE:

"Are you smaller than a goose?" → YES

"Do you eat meat?" → NO

"Do you live in my neighborhood?" → YES

"Are you brightly colored?" → YES

"Are you red?" → YES

"Are you a cardinal?" → YES!

PREDATOR-PREY HiDE-AND-SEEK

One person is the predator bird, and everyone else is the prey. Pick a place to be the "safe spot." The predator closes their eyes and counts to 10 while the prey hides. Now the predator goes on the hunt! The prey can escape by running, swimming, crawling, or flying to the safe spot before the predator catches them. The first animal to be caught becomes the next predator.

Here are some ideas:

PREDATOR	PREY
Owl	Mouse
Bald Eagle	Fish
Robin	Worm
Woodpecker	Beetle

PEREGRINE RACE

Line up next to a friend or two and pick a tree in the distance. Count to three, and then "fly" as fast as you can. The first to touch the tree is the fastest falcon!

Peregrine falcons are the fastest birds in the world!

Flocks of Birds

MANY TYPES OF BIRDS LIVE AND FLY IN GROUPS CALLED FLOCKS. Some groups stay together for short periods of time while looking for food. Others stick close as they travel long distances when the seasons change. Hundreds of birds can fly next to each other and make quick turns and dives without ever crashing into one another!

Canada Geese fly in V-shaped formations. They take turns flying at the front of the line.

Have you ever seen a huge **FLOCK** of birds overhead?

Can you run next to your friends without bumping into them?

It's easier to fly behind another bird.

When animals travel far during a change of season, it's called **migration** [my-GRAY-shun].

European Starling

Flocks of birds can be very noisy!

It's often easy to find a flock of pigeons in a city.

Herring Gull

Rock Pigeon

Zoom In

Notice if a flock flies in a line, a V, or some other shape. How many birds can you count?

HOW DO BIRDS FLY?

Most birds have lightweight bodies, strong chest muscles, and wings that are the right size to carry them.

Most birds begin to fly by flapping their wings as they jump into the air. Some birds need a running start to lift off.

Bird bones are hollow, like a straw, which makes them very lightweight.

Some birds can float on the wind to stay up in the air.

FLY LIKE A BIRD!

Look up in the sky. Do you see any birds flying? Pretend you're a bird and copy these flight patterns.

Flap your wings to a steady beat in a straight line *like a robin.*

Flap your wings then glide *like a hawk.*

Swoop up and down *like a finch.*

Hover over a pond *like a kingfisher.*

Soar and circle in the sky *like a vulture.*

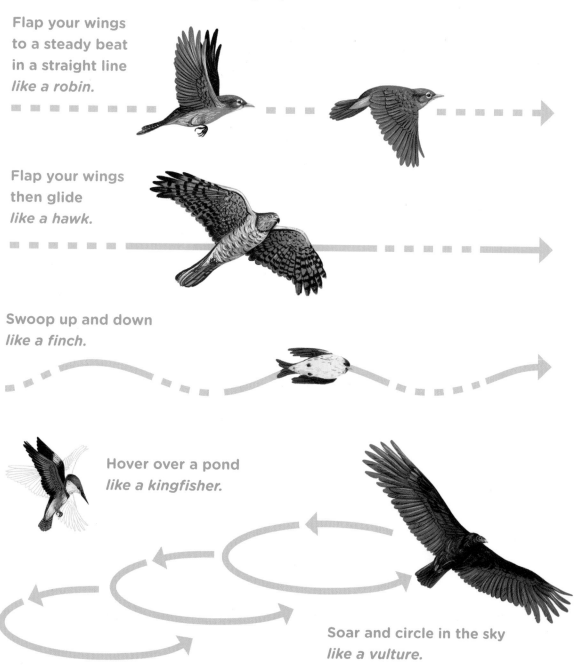

Bird Signs

I SEE IT!

LOOK FOR CLUES THAT BIRDS ARE NEARBY, EVEN IF YOU CAN'T SEE OR HEAR THEM. Check muddy patches of ground for footprints. Keep your eyes open for feathers. And be on the lookout for poop! Bird poop is usually white, but it can look black, purple, or green depending on what the bird ate.

Look for bird poop piled under a tree or splattered on the side of a building. There may be a nest above you!

Can you spot any of these **BIRD** signs?

Birds shed their feathers and grow new ones every year.

Hawk

Songbird

Heron

Crow

Bird footprints are called tracks.

Woodpecker

Gull

Hummingbird

Duck

Some people say it's good luck to be pooped on by a bird!

Zoom In

Owls swallow small prey whole, then spit out pellets full of the feathers, fur, and bones that they can't digest.

BiRD COUNT!

A **habitat** is a place where plants and animals live.
A good bird habitat provides food, water, and shelter.
**How many birds can you find in each of these
habitat pictures?**

Do you have
any of these
habitats
near you?

WOODLAND MEADOW

WETLAND

DESERT

BEHAVIORS!

Birds are always busy doing something! If you spot a bird doing one of these behaviors, check it off the list.

 SINGING ☐

 FLYING ☐

 PERCHING ☐

 FLOCKING ☐

 WADING ☐

 WALKING ☐

 NESTING ☐

 SWIMMING ☐

 FEEDING ☐